The May Anthologies were created two years ago as a forum for student writers at the beginning of their careers. Young writers face great difficulties in getting their early work published and it is the continued aim of these anthologies to provide an accessible platform from which young writers can reach a wide audience.

The great thing about this collection is that it demonstrates just how wide an outlook these writers have. Let us hope that this diversity continues. We would like *the May Anthologies* to grow to become a project that encompasses more writers from more universities.

Thank you to the writers and to the Executive Editors for their work, to the many colleges and individual financial contributors for their generosity and goodwill. Finally we would like to thank all those on the editorial committees and beyond, whose enthusiasm and commitment for the project – the production of the anthology itself – is so important.

Dorothea Gartland
Jason Thompson

D0765868

the May Anthology

of Oxford and Cambridge Poetry 1994

Varsity/Cherwell

First published in 1994 by Varsity Publications Ltd and
Cherwell.

ISBN: 0 902240 15 3

A CIP catalogue record for this book is available from the
British Library

Typeset in-house in Sabon by Varsity
Printed and bound by Ennisfield Print and Design,
Telfords Yard, 6-8 The Highway, Wapping, London E1 9BQ

Original concept: Adrian Woolfson, Peter Davies, Ron Dimant
Cover photograph: Jon Wright
Cover design: Ron Dimant, Sarah Lugg

Further copies of this book are available from good
bookshops in Oxford and Cambridge.

Editor: Dorothea Gartland (Cambridge)
Editor: Jason Thompson (Oxford)

Consultant editor: Bernard O'Donoghue

Publisher: Rebecca Thompson
Designer: Ron Dimant
Sub-editor: Raphael Lyne

Editorial committee:
Bill Davidson, Dan Davies, Elspeth Daya, Christine Hooper,
Jessica Lovell, Raphael Lyne, Tristan Marshall,
Vicky Moore, Kathy O'Grady, Ruth Scurr, Cathy Shrank

Editorial assistants:
Scott Boyd, Angela Clark, Patrick Mackie, Seamus Perry

Thanks to:
Nathaniel Grouille, Alan Hawkins, Emma Reddish

Cambridge College sponsors:
Clare, Corpus Christi, Downing, Emmanuel, Fitzwilliam,
Girton, Gonville and Caius, Jesus, Newnham, Pembroke,
Queens', Robinson, Sidney Sussex, Trinity

Oxford College sponsors:
Balliol SCR, Brasenose JCR, Christ Church JCR, Keble JCR,
Lincoln SCR, Lincoln JCR, Magdalen JCR, New College SCR,
Oriel SCR, Pembroke JCR, St Anne's JCR, St Catherine's JCR,
St Edmund Hall JCR, St Hilda's JCR, St John's SCR,
St John's JCR, Trinity SCR, Wadham SCR, Worcester JCR

Private donations:
Prof John Bayley, Ken Blakeson, Prof John Carey,
Miss E M Llewellyn-Smith, United Oxford and Cambridge
University Club

Contents

Introduction

At the launch of the Bloodaxe *New Poetry* last year, there were bitter complaints at the age cut-off point at fifty. Even the recent media-driven *New Generation* poets have an upper age limit of forty. Poetry publishing has a decidedly geriatric bias, which is surprising in view of the generally expressed neophilia in the discussion of it: 'the new rock 'n' roll', and so on.

It is therefore a rare and enlightening privilege to work on a project such as this anthology, to find out what *really* young people are writing about. What has struck me most is more evidence of how short a poetic generation is. I suppose I thought the kind of writing that might be expected to influence young poets would be the more avant-garde of the current established poets: the wry intimacy of Carol Ann Duffy or Jo Shapcott; the postmodern narratives of Paul Muldoon or Mick Imlah; the elusive sociology of Simon Armitage. There is remarkably little of any of that. Armitage comes to mind in 'Drinking' here, though it is much more focussed than he tends to be; 'Bare Foot' and 'The Locust Fields' have a Muldonian side to them: so has the light symbolism of 'Insect Radio'; and the intense superficial scrutiny of 'She Reached Down' has an air of Duffy to it.

But the differences from predecessors are much more striking, and more impressive, than the similarities. There were few extended narratives. The batch was remarkably unpolitical, tending more towards a cosmopolitan anthropology: a kind of obsessive antiquarianism as if the writers found more insight into the present human condition in aboriginal forms of society. Maybe it was a feeling of powerlessness that meant there was no mention of Yugoslavia and only one of Ireland (a domestic one in 'autumn'). If this generation of poets is to aspire to some kind of unacknowledged legislating, it will be by a decidedly oblique route. And fathers seem at last to be going out of fashion after a long innings.

On the whole the impression is of self-reliance. Most poems were in the first person. One beautiful poem – 'Watching Water' – even calls for a 'philosophical rationale' for this self-reliant inwardness. It should be said though that there were some powerful pieces of 'negative capability' too: the imaginative projection of 'Pea' and 'Winter Rain'. Of the signs of postmodernism, the most interesting is syntactic complexity, as in the mysterious 'Wren Burial' (with its inversion of 'Cock Robin') and the knotty 'Four Sonnet Season Sequence'. In the end the most convincing evidence of the enduring health of what was recently dubbed 'The Poetry Industry' was the secure survival of the attentive, linguistically scrupulous eye of the ageless poem, of which 'Toast' is a classic example.

As always, it is hard to suggest the full range in a short introduction. For example I haven't paid tribute to the formal skills on show, as in 'Lichas and Iole'. Given limitless scope, I would have itemised all the poems. But there are not that many, and I hope you find them all as absorbing to read as I did. They have my enthusiastic blessing.

Bernard O'Donoghue, March 1994

Drinking

Jamie Barras

My great great-grandfather, on the
Tyneside of the family, owned a
factory and drank. He drank wine,
whiskey, port and profits and they
buried him young, soaked in debt
and alcohol. In his redbrick glass
factory some of his workers spun
windows but most blew bottles,

turning them out for the breweries
that thickened the air on either
side with the dark promise of
fermenting hops. That promise
was the contract between yard and
ale; bottles clinked one way and
barrels rolled the other, their tapped
contents served up free to quench

the thirst of men tempered in the
dry heat of their workplace. That
thirst they carried with them on
past the factory gates into their
retirement, where, without
wages to pay for beer they used to
get for free, they took to milk for
health and economy. It was the

death of them. They daily worked
glasses rich in lead and breathed the
metal in. It swam in their blood
and settled in their bones,
accumulating, till, quenching their
thirst in the milk of retirement, they
sent calcium to their bones that swept
it out in lethal doses.

Retired glassblowers took to milk and
died of lead poisoning.

My great great-grandfather, on the
Tyneside of the family, owned a
factory and drank. He died of the
drink, they said, but if they'd asked
his workers they'd have told them,
over a beer, that it's not the drink
that kills you, it's the thirst.

Insect Radio

Jamie Barras

On the crest of Pontop Pike
satellite dishes multiply and grow
like turned mushrooms, wet with
the chitter-chatter of electronic
rain, and line-of-sight listeners are
caught in the shadow, the broad cast
of the radio mast that hums like
a plucked string poorly tuned
to stations too close together on the
dial to be separated by any stretched
wire aerial.

Up there transmissions ionise
the air and on still, humid summer
days that charged air lies wrapped
around the hill like the ghost of a
great worm.

Under its coils, pressed to the
ground by its weight, thousands
of flies and winged beetles crawl
with scattered ants in every direction
over the hard, grainy surface of the old
road, their wandering motion the
random noise, the chittering static of
insect radio.

It's a Long Stalk River that We Ride

Angela Clark

I felt,
standing there,
crackly feet on
hot rocks,
I felt
a countenance
if you can,
a solid sense
beyond my rolling
belly,
so,
as the heat
gave moisture
to the sky
and something
spat,

I stole
a paint rock
from
this beacon-eyed
lizard
who was
warming,
like me,
to the situation.

I took a paint rock
and sucked its roundness
for a coloured tongue
with which
to lick mine own face.

The markings stayed for days.

Bone Fire

Georgia Corrick

In spring the burnings hiss with sap,
and green wood cracks under the heat.
Those who die in spring are mostly old,
and new births fill their places:
we have few burnings in spring.
The plagues come in summer,
but by August the sun's too hot for fires,
and in autumn there seems so much to do,
a harvest to bring in, and eat.
You would think we had no fuel to spare
in winter, but they all bring logs;
the essential part is the stake.
I take a candle from the church,
and push dead leaves between the sticks
and light them. What else
should I do? I am their priest.

Four Sonnet Season Sequence

Kevin Cosgrove

1: "summer"

"ophelia dead in water, you asleep
in air. half waking as the moon just stares,
along the rivered land, at you. on hairs
of yours beneath a willow tree; a leap
of head to name that tree, as shadows creep
and eat all form until, at end, well there's
no shape at all but only shades and airs:
I can't now tell if tree you laugh or weep

at me. so slipping down, I go now down I do
beneath the muddied bank, in water, moons
I see all gathered up for me somehow

and turning round and looking up now through
the shallow tide I think the month of June's
light has arrived. but streetlamps orange now."

2: autumn

summer left withered trees and ashen boughs
no golden leaves but red wet rotting earth:
autumn came unexpected this year. vows
were made and broken for the foliage dearth.

but what was living is not yet in earth
instead it waits silent for November's fires
and the bright blaze of a new season's birth:
smoke crackle burns the flesh then leaves desires.

meanwhile in Ireland my grandmother tires/
grows ill. I write under a letter's stamp
this sonnet. and then I post it to her
so it reaches years too late that place damp.

I confess. I lost language. I was ill.
longing longing longing long longing still.

3: winter

winter saw me tripping down snowed-on hills
towards a frozen brook of ice mud fish.
behind the mound a clear sun winterkills
a now live-dead growth – go on extinguish

all this heap: was killed in autumn but stored
and burning now for pagan/christmas fuel.
the newly found heat is a treasured hoard
its suburban cityscape its bright jewel.

a motion rapidly pushed no friction
forwards under purple twilight/sunsets
onto adrenaline is no fiction
no mystics but skidding on ice. onsets

new sleep-fearing wake-loving. memory
returns. stars. eyes water: winter saw me.

4: spring

it has not yet come yet new life time
but its loveliness increases from cold
and soon its green and creature world foretold
will fill what is seen: metamorphose rhyme.
this season prophesied and promised prime
of all the others. for it, all was sold
and all awaited.

            the mud lifeless mould
shakes and separates. hands begin to climb,
six eyes reopen, nineteen fingers spread
a mythlike creature from a pool of piss
it is already living what was dead
and one thing one I extract from all this:

an empty tag but useful all the same
here there it is: "all things are not the same."

Poem to Philaenis

Lynn Dunlop

I must stop seeing rainbows
round the moon. It is a pursed
accusing mouth which throws

its twisted glares on our indifferent hands,
declaring witnessed kisses cursed.
A cold and clumsy light, it brands

our bodies with its lacerating stare
until our cheeks bloom ribbon-raw.
Only in darkness do we dare

to touch each other; and even there
when loved untraceably once, I saw
insistent rainbows flicker through the tear

in your closed curtains, and unwanted light
creep on the ceiling, with a surge
of sudden failure-fear. That was the night

your hair was full of hailstones
from the storm; and the conquered urge
to spell in the sky with my bones

the name which sings in every cell
was expressed as tears
when you did not agree to tell

this love I would stand in streets chanting
till insults were smiles.
For you would keep your cold gold ring

as fitted to the daily life which chokes
with safer fumes. Hardly surprising
that this talisman beguiles:
saving the lucent skin he never strokes.

Measures

Antony Dunn

(for Pamela)

Some things you can measure from the outset.
The magic of making our own ice cream,
the churn cold as milk under wet hands as
my thigh-backs barbecued against porchwood:
a rough number of turns, the strengthening
push of handle against palm, the dulling
of steel beneath condensation until
we couldn't quite see our faces in it,
the whispering of liquids and solids
becoming the slap of something other.

Years after my one visit to your home
a countdown which we could only measure
from its conclusion ticked softly into
life. And though there were still gradations and
weakenings and worsenings, the "only
x months to live" could be nothing more than
a vague hazard after a vague cell count.
Christmas Day: your son, my father, called me
to say we'd counted backwards to zero
from an at last finite infinity.

So when I think of you now it is in
measures – the number of steps between the
runway and your seat, the altitude and
distance over the Atlantic. How, with
your wheelchair stowed, you were as high and as
fast as anybody. How, flying west,
you must have wound back your watch those
                                        few hours –
time's wistful faux-ami. How many dark
cherries pressed onto a white cassata.
How cold the taste of our homemade ice cream.

Toast

Antony Dunn

Spitted on brass, floated over coals,
bread burns first around the crust – pale
squares with their dark frames of mundane
carcinogens;

like the black-edged envelopes which spoke
the "don't know how to say this" of
invitations to funerals,
or the other.

Sleeping Beauty Waking

Samantha Ellis

Pure ice I lie,
shut rosebud Isadora,
stifled by my pretty scarves
and at my fingertip
a drop of blood congealed;
a thorn has many names.

I am possessed by a wheel,
spinning,
a kind of strip roulette,
unravelling my shawl of old loves.
The players stack and count the chips
with jewelled hands and glares of pride.
So many of them!
Pretty coloured chips.

I crave heat;
the hands on my waist,
waltzing,
the chiffony moonlight.

The forest blurs and shifts in fog,
drunk princes leer towards the castle,
holding roses.

I shiver into warmth,
glass melting into skin.
My blood runs warm and stains the sheets.

Prince Charming leans above me,
proclaims his prize.
Parading pristine in the sun,
pure ice I smile –
my eyes are glazing over.

Winter Rain

E B Friedlander

Without warning,
Throughout the day

The ice melted,
Broken away

In nearly frozen water.
But cold repeats

Dreams of falling
From fences, seats;

Tripping on stairs,
Blossoms of sleep.

Bare Foot
Justin Frishberg

I came from a coffee shop
And as I walked down the street
I felt that the tarmac was hard on my feet
That grass would be softer
And I would walk bare foot
And as I walked down the street
The people around me
Were soon walking bare foot
And I smiled at all the toes that I saw
For many were short and stubby
Or had long unkempt nails
And many were handsome.

But as soon as the tarmac became grass
The street ended in a cliff
And I walked off the edge
And saw hollering faces behind me
Peering over the edge
Frozen in their silence
And more than I wanted to hear their screams
I wanted to know what they wore on their feet.

I looked below me to see where I fell
And I fell toward a rainforest
Green to the horizon
And I marvelled at the beauty
But realised that I was wrong
To marvel when I should have panicked
But before I could correct my mistake
And before I crashed into the forest
I was there
Amongst the leaves
Wet and green.

Not only was it luscious
But it was cold
And very noisy
Because though I could not hear the human screams
                                                    above
I thought I could hear the worm
Its segmented colon belching
And a black and yellow beetle
Thundering its legs against its shell
And a vole honking as it scurried
To a hole and underground
And despite myself I was there in the hole.

So I scraped against the soil
Because that's what voles do
And it was dark
And I could feel each grain of sand
Held by glistening balls of mud
Full with the earth and crumbled leaves
And the more I felt the ground around me
The more I went on
The more I could see
Until I bumped my head on a metal lid.

So I pushed up the lid of the hole
And I found myself in the tarmac of the street
And I could see the people looking away
Over the edge where I had gone
And they were still shouting
But I didn't tell them I was here
And I didn't join them in their screams
But laid the lid down gently behind me
And decided to walk home within myself.

Mayfly in Moscow

Justin Frishberg

Lermontov and I sat on the overnight train
From Leningrad to Moscow in April snows,
Taking vodka and bread to smooth the frosted track,
Philosophising over the breast of the femme fatale.

Through shaking window panes slid a frozen blue sea
Of timeless northern villages, existence their expression.
My mind slid on this glacier of studied superstition
To June in England and the meaning of the mayfly.

The mayfly, born Sunday dead Monday,
Spiralling between the two, furious to mate
Procreate so that others may take the challenge of life
And embellish the breeze, with a frenzy of flight

The human, spiralling between birth and death,
Religion and culture contorting our lives,
Desperate for meaning, in the creation of life
Desperate for solace, in the claw of the grave

The flight of the mayfly, blessed with a day
As strange as the stumbled history of man
Condemned to dust, to dust in the breeze
The breeze that frames the fury of the mayfly

As mayflies and sleep began to choke my tired mind
I shrunk into a depressed humility, asking
For a perspective that saved me from the dust
For God or the Devil, or for Fate to show herself.

Then a girl walked into my cabin and stared and sat
With thick-woven blue tights and thin white legs,
With orange hair in a ponytail
With a black velvet ribbon and a story.

There are giants who have feet to cross the earth,
And eyes that can see us though we can't see them.
And brains that men do not assign to giants
And the girl explained how they might think of us.

They see us, or ignore us, as we do mayflies;
They are either as men, floating in the breeze.
Or they are gods, the breeze their breath,
And we must hope their lungs are filled with charity.

And the girl left me with a smile and her story.
The faith that fate had a smile like hers
Eased me into a sleep of giants and mayflies
To wake the next dawn in Moscow's cold sun.

The Naming of Men
Richard Hansen

The room was dark. I fumbled for the light
but she said "Shh…". I found the bed

and stole inside, fearing
possession, Eden's shade where

she held me like a mud-spring.
She stumbled on my name.

I spluttered; "My name – my name –
what was it – no – it's gone."

"He's forgotten his name!" she said and laughed.
"Baptize me." I muttered. She waved her hand,

eyes strained for things forgotten
beyond her dancing fingertips, and said;

"Friend doesn't cover it –
you're not my lover –

are you, by any chance,
some kind of long-lost brother?"

Nameless, I can't stop giving names;

to mutilated dormice,
to bits of string and scraps of coloured glass.

I'm a child-changed patriarch
in a ruined baptistry.

Pea

Colette Harris

It is musty-moist in here.
I huddle, cuddled to my siblings.
Sunlight flickers over
the translucent veiny case that
holds us.

I am restless,
cramped by swelling rivals,
shuffling, endless quibblings,
drinking, drinking,
pushing, gleaming
round and smooth and plump.

Blind buds,
sickly, frail, sit futile at each end.

We are waiting, rustling
tense in this taut green calm.

Underwater light
washes our trembling home,
unreal,
bursting in this chloroform mist.
For what are we waiting?

We wallow in the lilting waves of
creeping warmth.
The lulling sun stirs the pod.
For what are we waiting?

She Reached Down
Judith Hudson

She reached down and touched the insides of her ankles.
They were cold.
When she was fifteen she had scratched the name of her
latest love
On her arm. With compasses.
Now she shuddered as she thought about blood poisoning.
She pulled the thin material taut across her legs
And hugged her calves,
Stroked the patterned surface; she liked to make her legs
disappear,
Swaddled down to the cold ankles.
Except sometimes, on the phone, in her dressing gown,
When she would stretch
And arc her legs around, wheeling, wheeling,
Like a synchronised swimmer on the duvet,
Admiring her bony knees.
The scars on her arms still showed sometimes under a tan,
And a mark on her finger where a knife slipped.

'Don't ask me to write about love...'
Greg Jackson

Don't ask me to write about love, I'm too tired
Tonight, too uptight, uninspired.
Too fired up to see clearly, too wired
To write more than her name. In a flash
Like a match flare it threatens to flame.
It's wrapped up, tightly packed up, intact
In my mind, but unwinds like a jack.

These days I keep things neatly locked up, up top,
Under wraps, and relax like a clock, no relapse.
Too much pain to transplant her name onto the page,
(All that rhyme and blind rage)
So I don't anymore.
Now writing's a chore that's ingrowing with age
Fuck it. I'll draw.

The Great Elegy for Brighton

Simon Jenner

This summer's a dead heat for nostalgia.
But the place I made a quarter century in
had its teeth cut in Regency, hollowed and gone
lushing its cropped spite till it yellowed gently.
House gaps stared, dentistry was metal houghing at the
                                                    years
like plaque, and finding them dead as nerves set alight.

Reeking its porcelain enlightenment, sparkling
a town of shells saltscoured like nightlife
so puffy in the aftertaste of coffee dawns,
and wicca women, so weird that they wanted me.
Our lusts were siliconed like years gone hard;
and lonely was an only tenderness, apart.

Young in a New Age, with its split ends of nostalgia
gazing into ragged amethyst
and materialist blown sapphires of Beetles, items
for the sleek amphetamines of Glastonbury.
The quartz is shaved into daylights.
For them the stone is worn down end to end.

Marrow is a food of anger, ebbing to
flutes or the sucked Tibetan pipes of the dead,
and firing out my roots with regrets
brittles me into whistling at noon.
This was a time of lovers into crystals
when all around salt sweated from the sea.

I can graunch at this shell that's Brighton in me,
a little flesh at the edges in a delicate twist
that says we're the sum of what our shelling wants.
Like the West Pier, that's a tangle of branches gone

rotten.
I've trodden very lightly when I've tripped on the

condemned,
steeped – over branches in reflection – roots fluttered in

blue soil.

A Prayer for Ellan Cain

Nick Kneale

We found your nameless grave, Ellan Cain,
Defiantly alive. Swaying in the saltwinds,
Grappled down the quartz of North Barrule
With blanched roots hard as knuckles,
Where the gabbling sea and mute church tower
For centuries have failed to drown your desire.

A voice in my veins said *you must be heard.*
It pumped me up the ribbed church steps,
Tunnelled me gently through arterial aisles
And out, from the knave and its Book of Births
Where I read your child's name, guttural and sure,
Eternally binding as an uncut cord.

A thick rain phlegmed from the mouth of Ramsey Bay.
It speared me with a new-born, ancient shame
As the memory screamed and once more took in breath
Of how the good folk here spat as you passed –
A woman, with child, without husband or land,
Belly-beached and heaving on the sharp shored Isle of Man.

And as damp birds were haemorrhaging from trees
I thought of you sweating, alone in wrenched labour,
Drawing light from your daughter through an unwindowed
winter,
To awake with the flowering on a clear April morning
When you walked the twelve miles from Jurby in a day
Chanting through clammed teeth *she shall have a name –*

From paddocks where the muscled bulls backed from your
stare,
Through pastures whose proud sheep bowed their double
horns,
And down along the no man's land of singing Sulby Glen
Where spirits danced beside you both to cheer you
On your way and irk the mainland priests
With songs no Christian ever played.

Clawing to that church, feet bloody as pig puddings,
You stain smeared across the glassy pricking floor,
Your will all consuming as though fire walking,
It cloaked you from the eyes of congregated burning
As the chosen jeered and sniggered at your pain.
And you gave your bastard child a Celtic name.

The Locust Fields

Tim Large

I

Some say there's
Ways to know they're

Coming: emu-magic,
Wheat-songs, a midge

In your left eye...
Year of the Blighters,

Tom saw the signs.
(He's an all-rounder:

Shears better than a barber,
Wraps a bale like it's

Your birthday). Tom's
Got psyku, sure as he's

Six-foot-four,
Never shaved in his life.

Will the harvest come
A cropper? Tom'll know,

Easy as swatting flies.
Time once he

Went shooting rabbits.
Comes back with his swag

And gun, says "How many
Rabbits in my sack?"

I wagered three,
Jo five; May guessed

None, reckoning he'd
Stuffed it with apples.

"Four and a half," says Tom,
And what do you know?

Four and one half,
Not a leg more, not an ear less –

He'd blown one
Clean through the hips.

II

First the willy-willy
Took his hat – chucked

It up from his head
Like the hat was a spigot

And Tom the fizz-bottle
That'd popped. So it

Swirls it round a bit
Like it's savouring the taste,

Sucks up other floatsomes too
(Jo's prescription, dust,

A scrap with a girl's number...)
Then it sets it

Down, gently as an angel
Hanging up wings.

Right on the highest chimney!
"Now," says Tom,

"That's a sign. Day
Chimney-pots hanker

To wearing hats, something's
Wrong." That night on Devil's

Elbow, Tom's engine
Blew and bandicoots flew out

With eyes: bandicoots,
Billows of them, swarming out

With fur, sparks and grumbling
To wake the Sleeping Sisters.

That's when the psykus got him
For sure – his crook gait

Nearly toppled him,
Rushing with the news.

III

Next few days, Devil days,
Hotter than Hell's breath…

Jo found religion.
He prayed more

Than a man's ever prayed:
Palms tight like he's

Caught in a clap, touching
His nose as though

To sneeze. (We'd no
Crucifixes on the farm,

But he made do with tongs
Opened wide to make

A kind of cross). Once,
He saw the Virgin Mary –

But it was Tom
Behind the drapes, closing

Windows to keep out flies.
May took to the Good Bottle.

Plumb in the paddock, singing
To the crops. She sang:

"The bunyip giveth, the bunyip
Taketh, rub-a-dub-dub..."

The psykus were strong
In us all, as we waited.

IV

Some say it's
The way of the land.

Buggered if I know,
But Tom's got a hunch –

Reckons a Great Wind
Painted like a rainbow

Once carved the valleys, deserts,
And the rivers too.

The rains filled its swathe,
Gushed down fishes and birds.

Then the animals came to drink
And the bush grew bigger.

Times it gets so thirsty
It sucks drought from the ground,

Or spits it all out
To make a big flood.

If that gale's belly
Strikes rock, fire leaps up,

Or else it sneezes, blowing
Blighters round the land.

Tom reckons this rainbow-wind
Does its crazy work

Till you don't know
What's what, but there's

A different colour
In every breath, and a new breath

In every throng.
I can only get wrapped

On simple things – May and me –
We danced in the paddock,

Tom and Jo played tunes
On sticks and kazoos.

V

Then they came. Like black
Gas jawing down,

Jeering, drifted on...
May didn't speak

For three, maybe four days –
Tom and Jo went

Bush awhile. I
Stood amongst stalks,

Where wheat had been,
Thought "There's ways

To know..." But the kookaburra
Was laughing. Some say

When it stops the silence
Is bigger than the sky.

Some say the land
Is like that. In the plucked

Field, long stalks
Ticking, a breeze, breathing...

I don't know...
On the horizon redgums

Held up the sky. And the sun
Blazed on stalks, fired

Shoots where the breeze
Went thwack, sucked

Dust where the willy-willy
Swirled, billowed it round.

A scrap of paper soared.
Surging from the dust,

A new bird with wings
Never known to people.

Lichas and Iole
Daniel Linstead

"Truly, it is her bad luck
that she cannot speak, but pardon her."

Dumbstruck from her fatherland
to a Sophoclean field;
translated from Oechalia
(where cities round her beauty fell),
in capture stands Iole.

Dark hair twists around her lips
windblown; her eyes entranced
with inner films of dissolution
and the hand which brought it
(intending to caress).

The spools unwind, rewind,
fidget through time and her life
like a tower, reintegrates
backwards, withdrawing desire
beyond the sweep of dust.

Iole's voice, caught in history,
cannot respond to questions
of her mother, of her husband
if she had one, and her name
seems unimportant.

The herald and the mute confront
across her silence and his speech
deceives her lover's wife to sorrow.
Lichas' tongue articulates
a space which is

the absence of their author.
Those who must lie together
under the sheets of one bed,
with the touch of one man,
exchange wordlessly until
the wife turns to Lichas,
who has spoken false,
and whispers "she
alone
knows how to feel."

Watching Water
Patrick Mackie

I

I could sit here all day,
    breathing in then out,
    I really could. The
    bluish afternoon
eases what little there
    is to say into
    a rush of feeling
    good about things and
watching. It's a strange world,
    watery and calm,
    there's no wind. I could
    sit here forever
and ever. Don't ask why.

II

There's a definite trick to it, just think
    of the water
    as a surface
for the light to toy with endlessly. Concentrate
    endlessly. Stick with one deep intricate
        patch until all
        else disappears
into the thought of watching water. Then listen
    to how quiet depth gets here, where the moment
        ripples, where the
        indefinite
surface shimmers the deliciously sinking sun.

III

What this world needs is a
  philosophical
  rationale for this
  sitting around, if
you want my opinion. So.

Wren Burial

Vesna McMaster

Bitter melancholy twists through the boughs on the
dying day of the year, and through the trees a column
of gaily dressed mourners. Bitter cold on the unsnowed,
frosted earth and the Piper at the head, cleaving the air.

Behind him the green-leaf bier: Black-veiled Queen
taps her fingers (a little impatiently) at the sixth attempt at a
lover born away. Robin beside her puffing out his red fat chest
and sitting on in regal warmth.

The Wren has died again who now lies stiff and belly
up, with blue frozen claws curled (one might think) in tiny
supplication; Robin cocks a merry eye, then glances at the
Queen.

The day of festivities over, the Night is natal to the Year.

Far more quick than thought the Ram, the Lion and the
Archer pass through their obedient marching town: new
harvest long gathered, and ploughed fields in states of brown
expectation.

A tearing noise commences in the silence.

Alone under the freezing myrtle, finding no refuge

on the crumbling earth, crouches Robin trembling:
At the end of his seventh year, wide-eyed and frozen-clawed
as he hears the hunting-cry not far enough, and the Piper
tuning up.

III: Bertrams Suburb
Adam Schwartzman

While the water tower squats like a Turkish bird
on the ridge and smiles more nicely the other way in green
and bougainvillaea to where the warmest houses face north,

the dead well-to-do are ignored and grumble in the plumbing.
This could be a local myth. There could be many.
Stark living rooms made to be seen into

stare at each other often across the streets and say secrets.
No brass and marble now. But it's more humbling
buying groceries on a teak floor and more like us

to prefer the peopled ruin. I see the gaping fanlight
in the hallway behind a fruit stall on the stoop
after rugby and now when it's dry and the roads turn back

to gravel into driveways, dust rises and sweet william and
anthracite
are there. There is a real side, where, when you never
stopped before,
you hear whispering on corners that only you understand.

from 'The Good Life, the Dirty Life'

V: The Sanctuary

Adam Schwartzman

(for Alice)

Our last big piece of free land frightens people.
The popular word is not to go to a place
that you don't know what can happen there.
For the time they are considered, the almost invisible
pedestrian myths that skirt it barefooted at twilight
are suspect. The rush hour returning bounce
light off his back and race up straight avenues
like tangents off a circle. In a while he turns
down where broad contours drain from under walls
of fortress communities into the stream park.
The ghosts of sleepers disappear in dry channels
as the next day unpresses dry grass. In years
his absence becomes only not being seen again.

from 'The Good Life, the Dirty Life'

His Love Comes Back with the Wind

Ruth Scurr

So suddenly Spain, on a London street,
Big boleroed into our lives,
And the wind, with the stars on string,
Embroidered over your eyes.
They were spangled, as a sequin cloth,
Bright in the ring before the bull comes in,
And though night cathedraled your voice so low,
Light eyes spilt a story through,
Intense as a stained glass window.

Shall I go to your chapel tonight?
Mantilla my mind to be humble before
The window of the woman you love?
Will I see you from the door, dancing on the floor,
Where the moon lies, telling the length of her,
And the colour, and the splendour, and the strength of her?
Will I grow dizzy from the sight of you
Swirling the cloak of her over your soul;
Will I press my eyes into my head, see nothing but red?

Biographies

Jamie Barras (Cambridge) was born and raised in the coalfields of County Durham and came to Cambridge in 1990 to study for a PhD in Physical Chemistry. He took up writing to entertain, to provoke and to pass the time while waiting for the day when he has more grey hairs than freckles.

Angela Clark (Oxford) was born in South Australia in 1971 and brought up in a commune on a rainforest mountain. From there she moved to a house by the sea in Sydney with her mother, brother and sister. Her education was traditional and it was whilst back-packing that she applied to New College, where she is now in her third year studying PPE. She edited the Oxford literary magazine, *Phoenix,* from 1992-93 and of writing says: "it's the dance of things – violent, sentimental, visual – that interests me most."

Georgia Corrick (Oxford) was born in 1973 and is currently studying English at Hertford College.

Kevin Cosgrove (Cambridge) is a second year English undergraduate at Trinity Hall. He is nineteen and lives in London.

Lynn Dunlop (Cambridge) was born in Scotland, is reading English at Downing College, and is happiest when surrounded by people, poems, cats and mountains. The title of her poem alludes to 'Sappho to Philaenis' by John Donne.

Antony Dunn (Oxford) is at St Catherine's College. He was born in London in 1973 and is now living in North Yorkshire. He was the winner of the 1992 Yorkshire Open Poetry Competition, judged by Dannie Abse. He also edited and contributed to a poetry anthology by students and staff from St Peter's School, York. *Burning the Old Boys* is published by Quacks/Purple Heart Publications. He has worked for Riding Lights Theatre Company in York, and represents musicians for Going Nowhere Management in London. His spare time is taken up by acting, and by singing and playing guitar for the Oxford band, Monkey Cage.

Samantha Ellis (Cambridge) is a first year English student at Queens' College. She lives in London and started writing when she was ten. She won the children's section of the Ouse Valley Poetry Competition and was a runner up in the W H Smith Young Writers Competion. She co-wrote a play, *You Startin'?* for a Freshers' Festival and is currently co-writing a second play, *The Nutter*, to be performed in Cambridge in November.

E B Friedlander (Oxford) graduated from Bennington College in 1991. He is currently on a leave of absence from St Catherine's College where he is a probationer research student. He lives in Stockholm where he works as producer and writer-in-residence for a modern dance company.

Justin Frishberg (Oxford) was born in Oxford and has lived there all of his life. He has, however, spent much time travelling in the USA as well as working there for a year with an environmental group. In his second year studying PPE at Balliol College, he received a rugby injury, in which he broke his neck and as a result is now confined to a wheelchair with tetraplegia. After a year of recovery and rehabilitation he is now back at Balliol, enjoying his studies and college life. He started writing only after his accident.

Richard Hansen (Cambridge) is a writer currently studying the canon of English poetry at Trinity College. His concerns include syntax and tonal ambiguity.

Colette Harris (Oxford) is a third year student of English Language and Literature at St Edmund Hall. She has been College Environment Officer and has participated in peer group support skills training to become a Student Advisor. She has also designed and created sets for productions of Ibsen's *Hedda Gabler* and Potter's *Blue Remembered Hills*. After vacation work experience with freelance writer Dr Rosalind Miles, she will be on a summer work placement with *Cosmopolitan* and ultimately hopes to pursue a career in creative writing.

Judith Hudson (Oxford) is twenty-one. She was born in Durham and has spent most of her life living in Newcastle-upon-Tyne. She is currently in her final year studying English at Hertford College.

Greg Jackson (Oxford) was educated at Wimbledon College and Westminster School sixth form, and is reading English at St Anne's College. He keeps goldfish and lives in Surbiton, Surrey.

Simon Jenner (Cambridge) was born in 1959, read English at Leeds and submitted for PhD at Robinson 'Deracinated Legacies: British Poetry of the 1940s', which together with an edition of one of the discussed poets – Drummond Allison – is published this summer. He is presently completing the first biography of diminutive 90s poet Lionel Johnson, and editing his work. Even more fun involves co-authoring a book on composite relationships in astrology. This poem's title derives from Brodsky's 'Great Elegy for John Donne'. It goes down badly in Brighton pubs, where its author has f/r/etched up despite himself. He describes himself as a literary sizist – drawn to poets under 5'4".

Nick Kneale (Cambridge) was born in Liverpool in 1966, although both his parents are from the Isle of Man. He is now doing a PhD in Victorian Decadent Literature at King's College, having studied English at York and Renaissance Drama at Warwick and the Sorbonne. Between studies he has lived in Paris and Italy, where he got married last year. They now live in Grantchester, but say they rarely have honey for tea at ten to three.

Tim Large (Oxford) was born in the USA in 1972, grew up in Adelaide, Australia, and now lives in Britain. He loves dancing and hitchhiking. He is currently a second year undergraduate studying English Literature at Balliol College.

Daniel Linstead (Cambridge) was born in London in 1972, and has lived resolutely in the same house ever since. After learning Sanskrit and Transcendental Meditation at school, he escaped South East England for travels in America, Europe and the Middle East, where he met the Bedouin but failed to discover himself. He is now in his final year reading English at Peterhouse, and shares rooms with a stuffed cheetah and a *Varsity* News Editor. He is curious about cinema, modern jazz, the ethics of backgammon, and his future.

Patrick Mackie (Oxford) is in his second year studying English at Worcester College. He writes for *Isis* and *The Word*, and his first play is currently being produced. He was born in London and supports Chelsea.

Vesna McMaster (Cambridge) was born in the town of Lublin in Poland and since then has led a migratory existence residing in Iran, Japan, Italy and finally the exciting town of Salisbury in deepest Wiltshire. She is now in her third year at Newnham College studying English. Her ambitions include being either poet laureate or a famous reporter.

Adam Schwartzman (Oxford) is a twenty year old South African in his first year reading English at Pembroke College. He has had work appear in the *Independent*, *PN Review*, *Verse*, as well as other publications in the UK, South Africa, France and Australia. Some of his poems appear in the anthology *New Poetries* (Carcanet) and his first collection will be published by Carcanet in May 1995. For 1996 he is editing a Carcanet anthology of New South African poetry. He is one of the editors of a University Arts magazine, *Caroboree*, writes regularly for *The Word* and is involved in restarting the Oxford Poetry Society.

Ruth Scurr (Cambridge) was born in London in 1971, daughter to John and Gillian Scurr, and was educated at St Bernard's Convent, Slough and Mansfield College, Oxford. She is currently studying Political Thought in Cambridge.